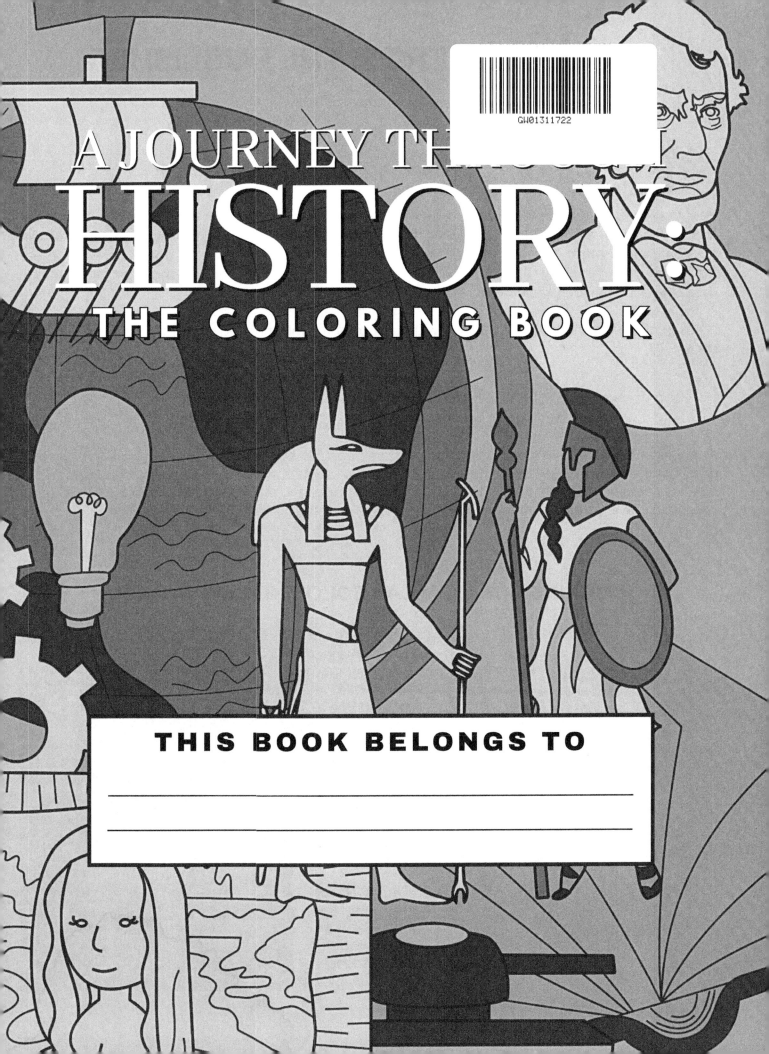

A MESSAGE FROM THE PUBLISHER

Hey, thank you for making the purchase, we really hope you enjoy this book. If you have the chance, then all feedback is greatly appreciated. We have put a lot of effort into making this book, so if you are not completely satisfied, please email us at ben@bclesterbooks.com and we will do our best to address the issues. If you have any suggestions, enquries or want to send us a selfie with this book, then email at the same address - ben@bclesterbooks.com

Is this book misprinted? Drop us an email with a photo of the misprint and we will send out another copy!

WHO ARE WE AT B.C. LESTER BOOKS?

B.C. Lester Books is a small publishing firm of three people based in Buckinghamshire, UK. We aim to provide quality works in all things geography, for kids and adults, with varying interests. We have already released a selection of activity, trivia and fact books and are working hard to bring you wider selection. Have a suggestion for us? Then email ben@bclesterbooks.com. We are all ears!

LOOKING FOR A SIMILAR COLORING EXPERIENCE?

Color in some of the most well-known landmarks of the world, from Big Ben to Sydney Opera House!

Unwind, relax, and bring some of our planet's most beautiful natural scenery to life with color!

BEFORE YOU START...

Test your coloring equipment here for bleedthrough. Note that this coloring book is NOT recommended for paint, gel pens or highlighters...

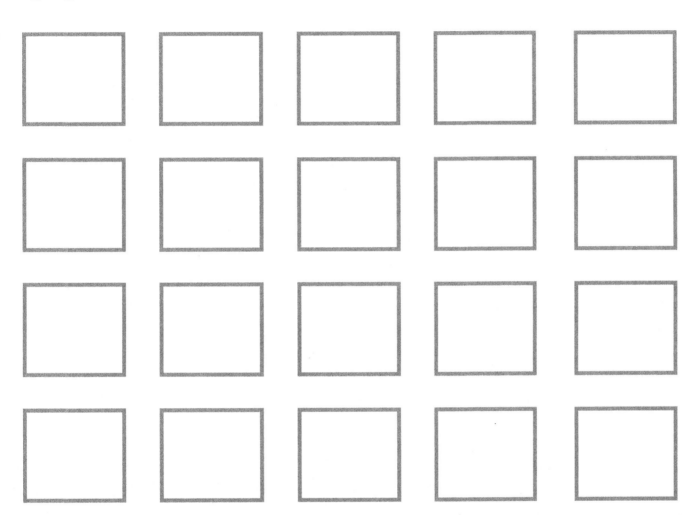

Visit us at www.bclesterbooks.com for more!

No part of this book may be copied, reproduced or sold without the express permission from the copyright owner.

Copyright B.C. Lester Books 2021. All rights reserved.

READY TO START?
Relax, unwind, and enjoy the experience!

Stone Age

Stone Age

Ancient Egypt

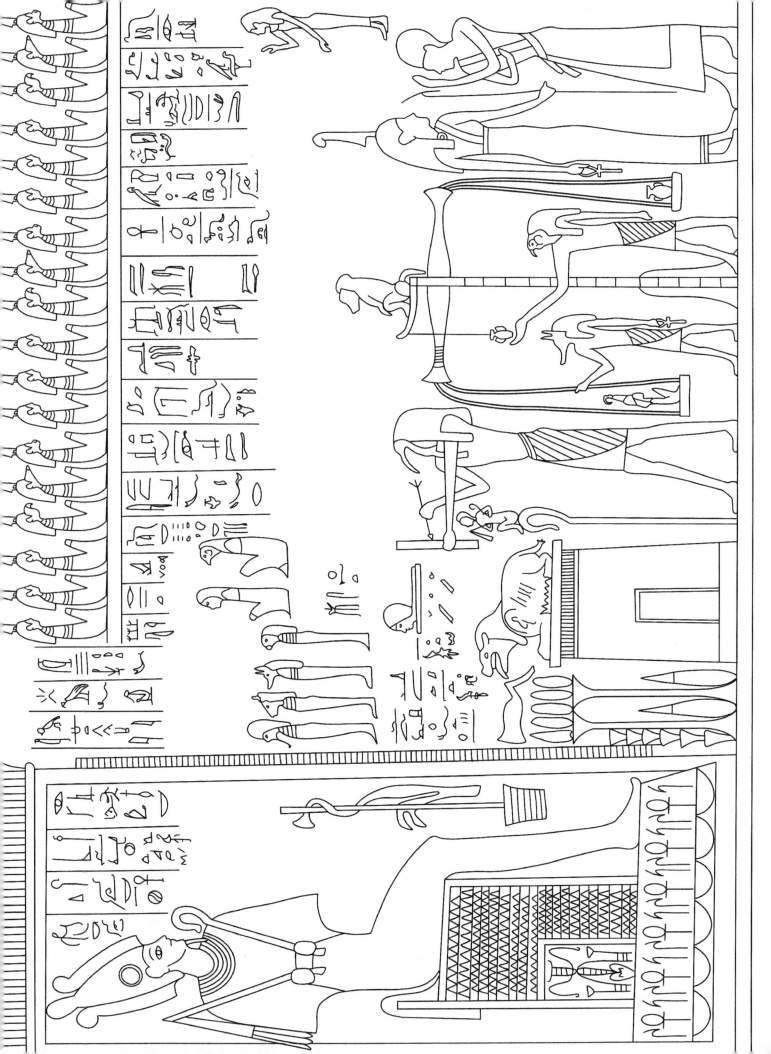

Ancient Egypt

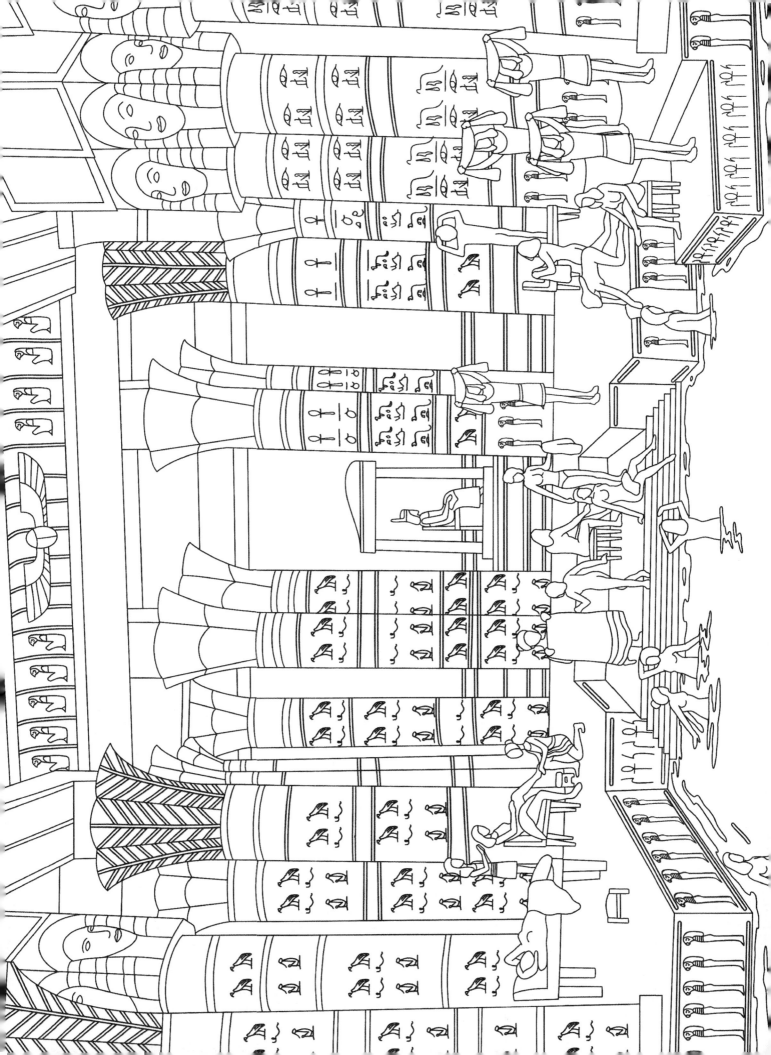

Ancient Rome

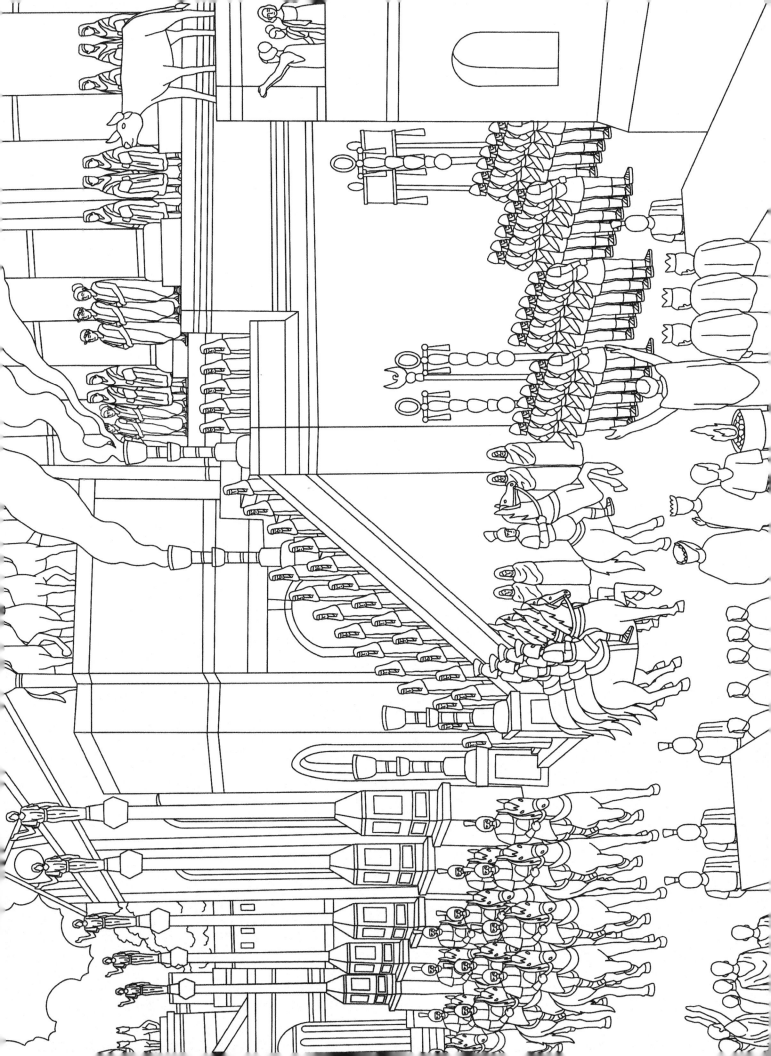

Ancient Rome

Vikings

Vikings

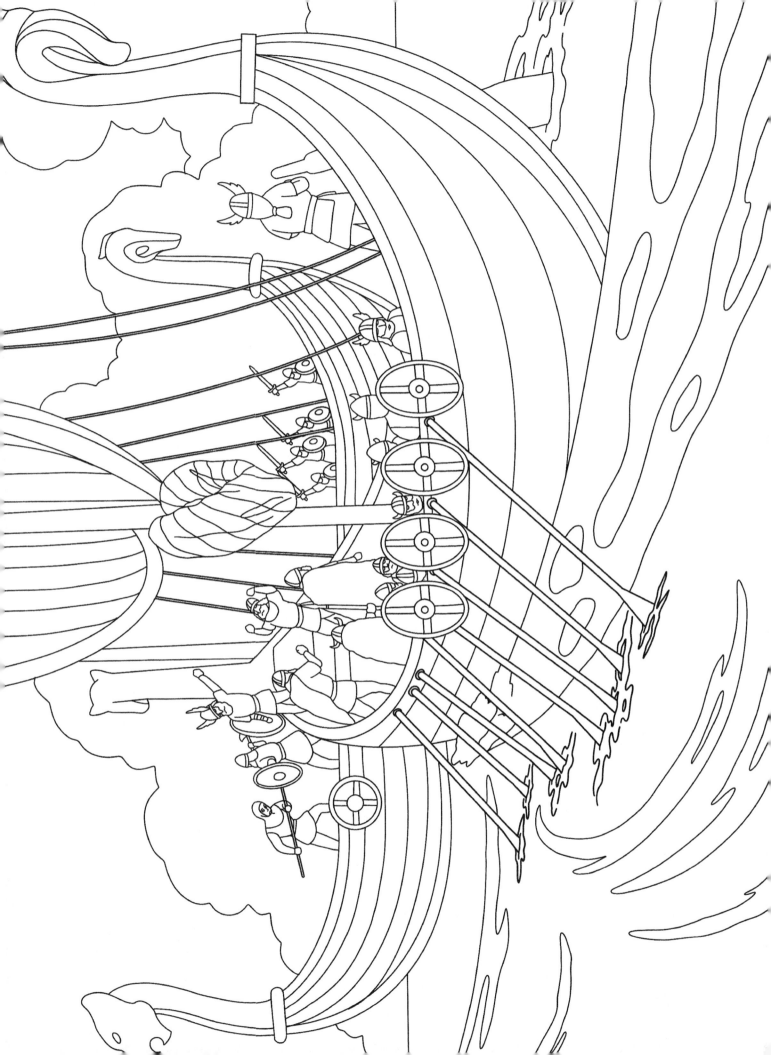

Crusades

Crusades

Tudors

Tudors

Renaissance

Renaissance

Industrial Revolution

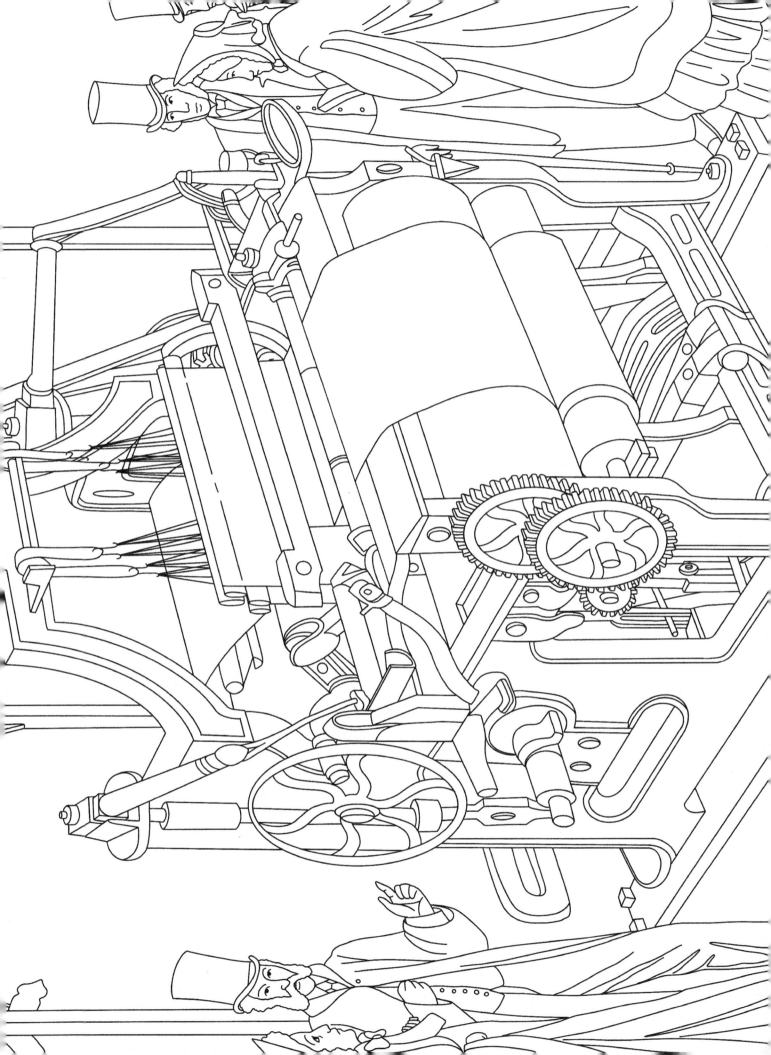

Industrial Revolution

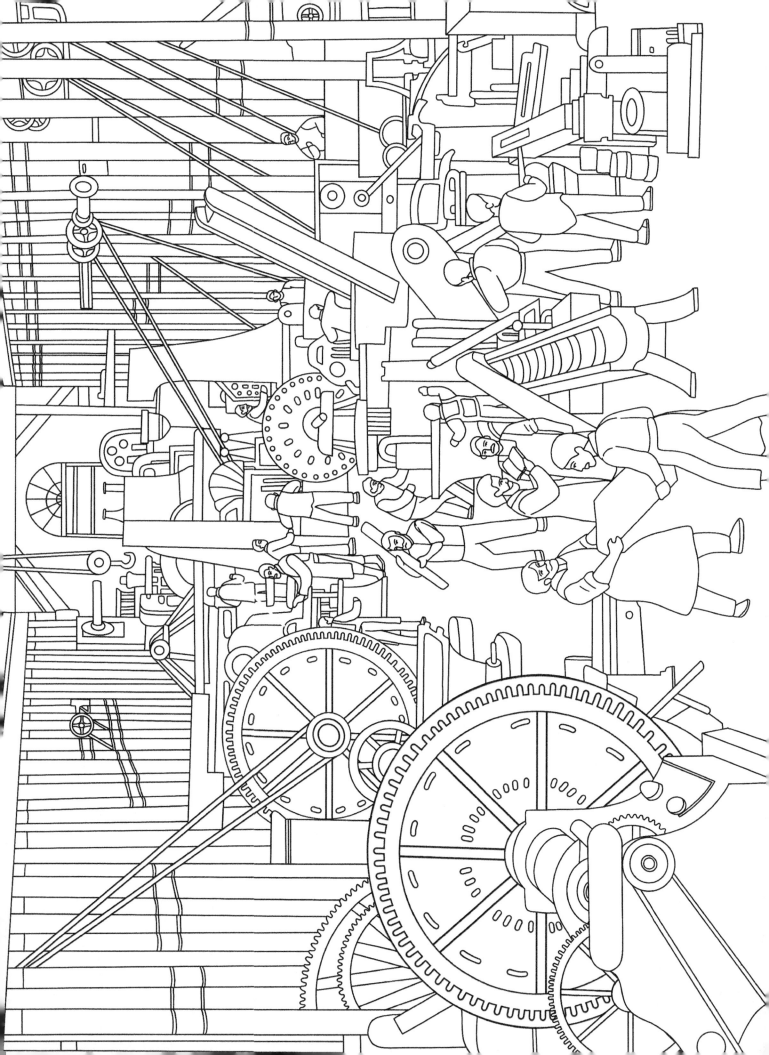

American Revolutionary Wars

American Revolutionary Wars

Victorian Era

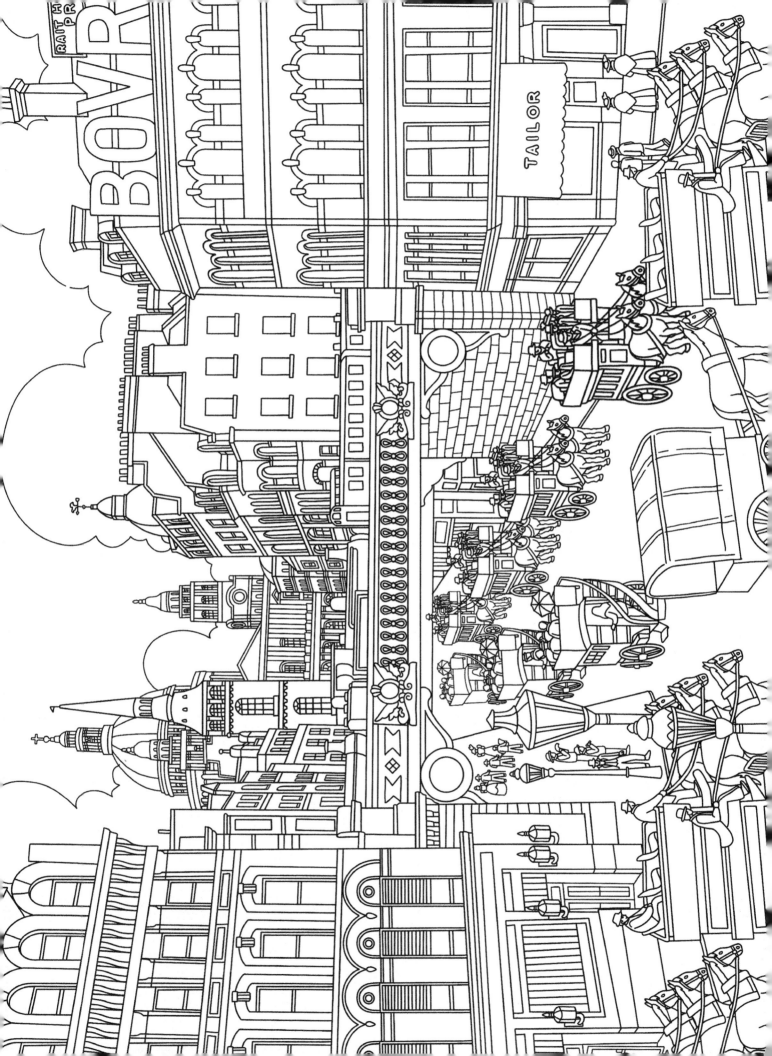

Victorian Era

American Civil War

American Civil War

Heroic Age of Antarctic Exploration

Heroic Age of Antarctic Exploration

World War I

World War I

World War II

World War II

Cold War

Cold War

Printed in Great Britain
by Amazon